PEAKS, PLATEAUS & CANYONS
OF THE
Grand Circle

Impact, 4961 Windplay Drive, El Dorado Hills, CA 95762

PEAKS, PLATEAUS AND CANYONS OF THE
Grand Circle

Photography provided by Terry Donnelly, Mark Henderson, Dai Hirota, Gary Ladd, David Muench, Tom Rickets/ Dinosaur National Monument, Jerry Sieve, Tom Till, Larry Ulrich and John Wagner

Illustration provided by Impact Photographics

ISBN: 1-60068-027-5

First Printing, December 2007

4961 Windplay Drive, El Dorado Hills, CA 95762
www.impactphotographics.com

Printed in China

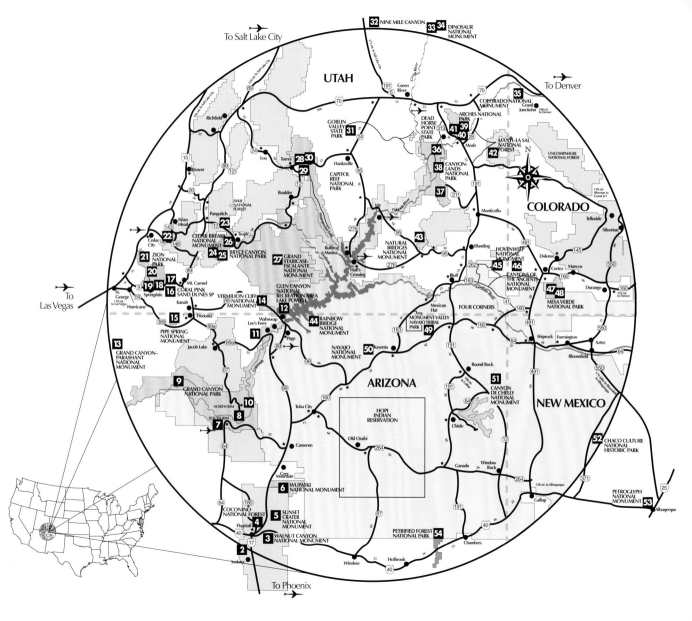

Cathedral Rock, Coconino National Forest, Arizona
The Coconino National Forest is one of the most diverse national forests in the country, with landscapes ranging from the famous red rocks of Sedona to ponderosa pine forests and alpine tundra.

Walnut Canyon National Monument, Arizona

The presence of water in a dry land made the Walnut Canyon rare and valuable to its early human inhabitants more than 700 years ago. Remnants of the early settlers' lives are preserved here, through the efforts of the U.S. Forest Service, the National Park Service, and other public agencies. The monument remains valuable today as habitat for plants and animals.

San Francisco Peaks, Coconino National Forest, Arizona
Rising above Flagstaff, the San Francisco Peaks mark the highest point in Arizona at 12,633 feet. Many geologists believe that the multiple peaks are the remnants of a single stratovolcano that erupted with explosive force more than 100,000 years ago, much like Mount St. Helens did in 1980.

Sunset Crater National Monument, Arizona
Sometime between A.D. 1040 and A.D. 1100, a series of eruptions built the tall cinder cone of Sunset Crater. Undoubtedly witnessed by native people, the lava flows and fallen cinders profoundly affected their way of life. Now, this volcano and its surrounding landscape provide an unparalleled opportunity to study plant succession and ecological change in an arid volcanic landscape.

Lomaki Ruin, Wupatki National Monument, Arizona
Lomaki is one of many Ancestral Puebloan dwellings preserved at Wupatki National Monument.
Using tree-ring dating and other archeological evidence, we now know that as many as 3,000 people
occupied Wupatki at its height, between A.D. 1130 and A.D. 1160, farming and gathering native plants and
animals in a difficult land with little rainfall.

South Rim, Grand Canyon National Park, Arizona
Even before it was established as a national park in 1919, the Grand Canyon attracted the curious and adventurous from all over the world. Today, this breathtaking canyon continues to remind visitors of nature's awesome power.

North Rim, Grand Canyon National Park, Arizona
Located entirely in northern Arizona, the park encompasses 277 miles of the Colorado River and 1.2 million acres of adjacent uplands. One of the most spectacular examples of erosion anywhere in the world, the Grand Canyon offers incomparable vistas to visitors on the rim. Grand Canyon National Park is a World Heritage Site.

Toroweap Overlook, Grand Canyon National Park, Arizona
The view from Toroweap Overlook, 3,000 vertical feet above the Colorado River, is breathtaking; the sheer drop, dramatic! Equally impressive are the volcanic features, cinder cones, and lava flows, which make this viewpoint unique in Grand Canyon National Park. Renowned Lava Falls Rapid is just downriver and can easily be seen and heard from the overlook.

Nankoweap Granary, Grand Canyon National Park, Arizona
Though the Grand Canyon's geology often eclipses its cultural history, the canyon and surrounding rims
are virtually littered with evidence of human habitation dating back 12,000 years. The storage niches at
Nankoweap are accessible only from the river or the demanding Nankoweap Trail.

Colorado River, Grand Canyon National Park, Arizona
Shaped by the erosive power of the Colorado River, the majestic Grand Canyon stretches 277 miles from end to end, averaging 10 miles wide and one mile deep. Of this intricate natural wonder President Theodore Roosevelt once said that it is "the one great sight that every American should see."

Glen Canyon National Recreation Area, Utah

Glen Canyon National Recreation Area consists of 1.25 million acres of land and water with miles of red rock canyons bordering the crystal waters of Lake Powell and the Colorado River. Eighty-seven percent of the recreation area is dry land above Lake Powell and offers desert hiking and backcountry adventure.

Grand Canyon–Parashant National Monument, Arizona

Grand Canyon–Parashant National Monument covers more than one million acres of the Arizona Strip, an area often described as "high, dry, and lonesome." The monument contains valuable resources that offer a clear view to understanding the geologic history of the Colorado Plateau.

Vermilion Cliffs National Monument, Arizona
Brilliant red cliffs flank the southern edge of the Paria Plateau, west of Page and north of the Grand Canyon.
A geologic treasure, this area also became a popular route for many historic expeditions. Endangered
California condors were reintroduced here in 1996, and continue to thrive in this remote terrain.

Winsor Castle, Pipe Spring National Monument, Arizona
Completed in 1872, Winsor Castle is one of the primary attractions of Pipe Spring National Monument,
Arizona. This Mormon settlement was built on the traditional homeland of the Kaibab Paiute Tribe
and typifies the struggle between two cultures.

Coral Pink Sand Dunes State Park, Utah
Rippling arcs of coral-colored sand cover nearly 4,000 acres of southwestern Utah. Here, stunning dune fields are surrounded by red sandstone cliffs, blue skies, and pinyon-juniper woodlands in a kaleidoscope of color.

Zion National Park, Utah
An expanse of cross-bedded Navajo Sandstone is punctuated by pine trees near the Zion–Mt. Carmel Highway in Zion National Park's eastern highlands.

Zion Canyon Overlook, Zion National Park, Utah
The hike to the top of Zion Canyon Overlook includes stunning views of East Temple, Towers of the Virgin, and the Streaked Wall. Hikers often sit among the nest of hoodoos at the end of the trail gazing down into lower Zion Canyon at the twists and turns of the Zion switchbacks.

The Watchman, Zion National Park, Utah

The Watchman, a monolith of Navajo sandstone, is a prominent landmark near the mouth of Zion Canyon in Zion National Park.

The Narrows, Zion National Park, Utah
The Virgin River, in Zion National Park, continues to shape the landscape, removing more than a million tons of rock and sand each year. Once a tributary to the Colorado River, the Virgin now flows into Lake Mead, the reservoir that formed behind Hoover Dam.

Kolob Canyons, Zion National Park, Utah
The 1,500 foot walls of the Kolob Canyons glow in the late afternoon sun. Located in the northwest corner of Zion National Park, these canyons provide a colorful panorama of some of southern Utah's best red rock scenery.

Cedar Breaks National Monument, Utah

Resting atop the Colorado Plateau, at an elevation of over 10,000 feet, this breathtaking view awaits. Millions of years of sedimentation, uplift, and erosion are carving out this giant amphitheater that spans some three miles, and is more than 2,000 feet deep. Due to minerals that have been deposited over time, the cliffs of Cedar Breaks National Monument display an amazing rainbow of warm hues.

Red Canyon, Dixie National Forest, Utah
The Dixie National Forest is the largest national forest in Utah, with two million acres spanning 170 miles across the southern part of the state. It is a land of varied terrain, from sparse deserts to alpine forests, and contains the variety of plant and animal life that inhabits these diverse climate zones.

Thor's Hammer, Bryce Canyon National Park, Utah

Located down the Navajo Loop trail is Thor's Hammer which peeks up above the rest of the hoodoos at Sunset Point. Erosion has carved the colorful limestone and sandstone formations into spires, fins, and arches, now referred to as hoodoos.

Bryce Amphitheater, Bryce Canyon National Park, Utah
Virtually all of Bryce Amphitheater can be seen from the rim at Sunset Point. It is a view of what is perhaps
the most breathtaking maze of erosional forms on Earth—the Silent City.

Natural Bridge, Bryce Canyon National Park, Utah
Natural Bridge is actually a window formed by frost-wedging. Bryce Canyon experiences over
200 freeze/thaw cycles each year. As winter snow melts, water seeps into the cracks and freezes at night,
expanding by almost 10 percent. Expansion forces the cracks to become wider and wider, eventually
creating a significant opening.

Grand Staircase–Escalante National Monument, Utah

This high, rugged, and remote region of southern Utah is an unspoiled expanse of bold plateaus and multi-hued cliffs stretching for untold distances. Its relatively untouched nature makes it a rich laboratory for scientific and cultural studies.

Chimney Rock, Capitol Reef National Park, Utah
In the continuing saga of nature, Chimney Rock stands as a sentinel along Highway 24 in Capitol Reef
National Park. The soft 550 foot Moenkopi pedestal is protected by a more erosion-resistant Shinarump cap.

Fruita Historic District, Capitol Reef National Park, Utah

In the late 19th century, hardy Mormon farm families settled the area that eventually became know as Fruita. The Pendleton-Gifford barn, built by Calvin Pendleton, is situated in the heart of Capitol Reef National Park and is a key element of the Fruita Rural Historic District. The Pendleton-Gifford barn is listed on the National Register of Historic Places.

The Castle, Capitol Reef National Park, Utah
Colorful sedimentary rock layers of Capitol Reef National Park are easily visible at The Castle and all along
the cliffs of the Waterpocket Fold, a 100-mile-long warp in the earth's crust.

Goblin Valley State Park, Utah

Goblin Valley State Park is inhabited by strange and unique rock sculptures carved by wind and water,
which suggest mischievous goblins and phantasmagoric creatures. It also contains colorful chocolate-colored
balanced rocks, spires, and pedestals amidst the solitude of the San Rafael Desert.

Hunter Panel, Nine Mile Canyon, Utah
Nine Mile Canyon is an outdoor museum of Fremont Indian pictographs and petroglyphs created more than a thousand years ago. Because of its relative isolation and dry climate, the canyon and its treasures remain much as they were hundreds of years ago.

Echo Park, Dinosaur National Monument, Utah

Soaring above the gleaming confluence of the Green and Yampa rivers, Steamboat Rock marks the heart of Echo Park. An early conservation battle was fought, and won, here in the 1950s with the defeat of a dam project that would have flooded this sandstone canyon and turned Steamboat Rock into a tiny island.

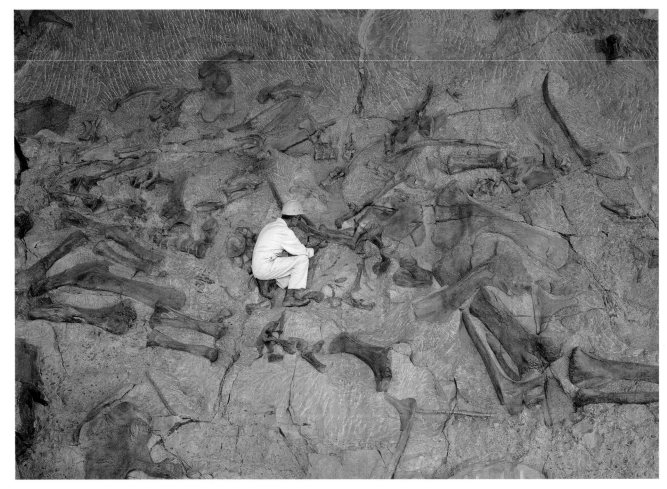

Dinosaur National Monument, Utah
Dinosaur National Monument protects one of the richest fossil deposits in the world. Here paleontologist Tobe Wilkins, veteran of 30 years of quarrying, carefully chips rock away to expose fossil dinosaur bones.

Monument Canyon, Colorado National Monument, Colorado
Established in 1911, Colorado National Monument was the first national monument designated in the state of Colorado. It was established to preserve and interpret outstanding geologic formations as seen from the historic Rimrock Drive.

Dead Horse Point State Park, Utah
Located on a sheer-walled narrow peninsula that juts 2,000 feet above the winding Colorado River, Dead Horse Point State Park provides breathtaking views of southeastern Utah's canyon country. It was established in 1959, covers an area of 5,082 acres, and is commonly referred to as "Utah's Grand Canyon."

Needles District, Canyonlands National Park, Utah
Named for the colorful spires of Cedar Mesa Sandstone that dominate the area, the Needles District forms
the southeastern corner of Canyonlands National Park. Foot trails and primitive roads provide many
opportunities for long day hikes and overnight adventures.

Island in the Sky, Canyonlands National Park, Utah
Canyonlands National Park preserves 527 square miles of colorful sandstone canyons, mesas, buttes, fins, arches, and spires in the heart of the Colorado Plateau in southwestern Utah. Water and gravity have been the prime architects of this land, carving flat layers of sedimentary rock into the landscape seen today.

Delicate Arch, Arches National Park, Utah

In Arches National Park, the forces of nature have, over an immense span of time, created a wondrous landscape. Folds and warps in the red sandstone layers indicate movement of long-buried salt deposits. Hiking trails lead to graceful spans arcing against the sky, enormous rocks balanced on thin spires, standing rock fins, and cliff walls hundreds of feet high.

Turret Arch, Arches National Park, Utah

Turret Arch is named for the tower which ascends from one end of this distinctive feature. This arch, found in the Windows Section of the park, actually consists of three openings, the largest measuring 35 feet wide and 65 feet high. The park preserves over 76,000 acres of unique geological resources and formations. In some areas, faulting has exposed millions of years of geologic history.

Balanced Rock, Arches National Park, Utah

A remarkable feature of the park, Balanced Rock is precariously perched and seems to defy gravity. It is composed of the Slickrock Member of Entrada Sandstone forming the harder cap rock and the Dewey Bridge Member of the Carmel Formation forming the more quickly eroding base. Arches was established as a National Monument in 1929 and designated as a National Park in 1971.

Haystack Mountain, Manti–La Sal National Forest, Utah
Peaking at 11,642 feet above sea level, Haystack Mountain offers expansive vistas of the entire
Canyonlands region and provides a cool retreat from the heat of nearby Colorado Plateau deserts.
It is particularly attractive in autumn when its slopes become a mosaic of color.

Owachamo Bridge, Natural Bridges National Monument, Utah
At an elevation of 6,500 feet, pinyon and juniper-covered expanses of Cedar Mesa Sandstone are etched with deep canyons carved by meandering streams. Where streams cut through sandstone walls, three large natural bridges formed.

Rainbow Bridge National Monument, Utah
Rainbow Bridge is the world's largest natural bridge, measuring 290 feet high and 275 feet wide. First viewed by Anglos in 1909, neighboring Indian tribes have long considered it to be a sacred religious site.

Hovenweep Castle, Hovenweep National Monument, Colorado-Utah Border
Six remote Ancestral Puebloan-era villages are spread along the twenty-mile expanse of mesa tops protected within Hovenweep National Monument. Evidence of human use dates back 10,000 years to a time when nomadic Paleo-Indians hunted and gathered food in this area.

Painted Hand Pueblo, Canyons of the Ancients National Monument, Colorado
The unique 13th-century towers in this region might have been homes or defensive structures or used to observe the landscape, sun, and night sky. The rugged landscape includes traces of Ancestral Pueblo, Ute, Navajo, and historic pioneer settlements.

Spruce Tree House, Mesa Verde National Park, Colorado

Spruce Tree House, one of the largest and best preserved pueblos in Mesa Verde National Park, was one of the first dwellings to be excavated in 1908. These sites are some of the most notable and best preserved in the United States.

Cliff Palace, Mesa Verde National Park, Colorado
Designated in 1906, Mesa Verde was the first national park established to preserve the works of Ancestral Puebloans. From approximately A.D. 600 to A.D. 1300, people lived and flourished in communities throughout the area, eventually building elaborate stone villages in the sheltered alcoves of canyon walls.

Monument Valley Navajo Tribal Park, Utah
The stately monoliths, red buttes, arches, and sand dunes of Monument Valley are located within Navajo tribal land and were made famous by western movies filmed in the area.

Keet Seel Ruin, Navajo National Monument, Arizona

Navajo National Monument protects three of Arizona's largest cliff dwellings: Inscription House, Betatakin, and Keet Seel. One of the West's best-preserved Ancestral Puebloan dwellings, Keet Seel contains more than 160 rooms and four kivas in a large sandstone alcove. Once home to over 150 people, Keet Seel was only briefly occupied and stood empty by A.D. 1300.

Spider Rock, Canyon de Chelly National Monument, Arizona

At the base of sheer red cliffs and in canyon alcoves are remnants of prehistoric dwellings built between A.D. 350 and A.D. 1300. Canyon de Chelly National Monument offers visitors the chance to learn about Southwestern Indian history, from the earliest basket-makers to the Navajo Indians who live and farm here today.

Pueblo Bonito, Chaco Culture National Historical Park, New Mexico
Chaco Culture National Historical Park preserves one of America's most significant cultural and historic
areas. Pueblo Bonito is the most thoroughly investigated and celebrated cultural site in Chaco Canyon.
Planned and constructed in stages between A.D. 850 to A.D. 1150 by Ancestral Puebloan people,
this was the center of the Chacoan world.

Petroglyph National Monument, New Mexico
Petroglyph National Monument protects a variety of cultural and natural resources, including volcanoes,
archeological sites, and an estimated 20,000 carved images. Many of the images are recognizable as animals,
people, brands, and crosses; others are more obscure. These images are inseparable from the cultural
landscape and the spirits of the people who created them.

Petrified Logs, Petrified Forest National Park, Arizona
Petrified Forest National Park was established to protect a rich deposit of fossils from a Triassic-Period ecosystem. Quartz and trace minerals have replaced the original wood of ancient trees, creating a delicate rainbow of color that is surprisingly hard and resistant to erosion.